Trading BITCOIN

From Earth to the moon!

Franklin Schimidt

Copyright © 2024 by Franklin Schimidt
All rights reserved.

No part of this book may be reproduced, distributed, or transmitted in any form or by any means, including photocopying, recording, or other electronic or mechanical methods, without the prior written permission of the publisher, except in the case of brief quotations used in reviews or other non-commercial uses permitted by copyright law.

This book is intended for informational and educational purposes only. The author is not a financial advisor, and the contents of this book should not be considered financial or investment advice. Readers are encouraged to consult with a professional advisor before making any financial decisions.

First Edition
ISBN: 9798346286295
Imprint: Independently published

Contact the author drfgs@hotmail.com

About The Author

Franklin Schimidt is a passionate Bitcoin trader and educator who discovered cryptocurrency in 2013 and never looked back. With a background in economics and years of experience in both traditional and digital finance, Franklyn specializes in simplifying complex financial topics for beginners. His mission is to empower others to navigate the world of Bitcoin safely and profitably. "Trading Bitcoin for Doomies! From Earth to Moon!" is his debut book, created to make Bitcoin accessible to everyone.

Intuition and Reason

in Trading

This manual was created to help beginners navigate the fascinating world of Bitcoin, offering guidance on how to buy, store, and profit safely. However, it's important to note that it's not meant to replace your personal intuition.

When it comes to investing, human intuition plays a fundamental role alongside reason.

How Intuition Works in Decision-Making?

Intuition is like an internal guide. It's shaped by our experiences, perceptions, and even instincts. Often, it's that "gut feeling" we have about what to do, even when there isn't a logical explanation. In trading, this intuition might be a subtle warning that something feels off, or it might add extra confidence in a particular decision. It's fueled by accumulated knowledge and experience over time.

Reason, on the other hand, is the use of logical thinking and data to make informed decisions. In Bitcoin trading, this means analyzing charts, keeping up with the market, and understanding the risks and rewards.

Reason helps maintain focus, avoiding impulsive decisions driven by emotions.

Balancing Intuition and Reason:

Just like a pilot who relies on both instruments and instinct, a Bitcoin trader should balance intuition with reason. This book provides tools and information to support your journey, but it's up to you to listen to your intuition and apply rational thinking to make the best decisions.

Important Disclaimer

Bitcoin is a high-risk investment, and the market can be extremely volatile. This manual serves as a guide, but remember: the final decision is always yours. Use intuition as a complement to reason and knowledge, and take responsibility for your choices.

With this balance, you'll be more prepared to explore the Bitcoin market safely and responsibly. Enjoy the reading, and happy trading!

Is Bitcoin a Scam?

To answer the question, "Is Bitcoin a scam?" let's consider another question: "Is money real?" After all, what makes something considered "money"? Let's go back in time to understand this concept.

From Barter to Modern Money

Before money existed, people traded what they had directly for what they needed. This system, known as bartering, worked well in small communities where needs were simple, and value was directly tied to each item's usefulness.

For example, a farmer with wheat might trade with a fisherman for fish. But there was a problem: the fisherman might not always need wheat at that moment, making direct trades difficult. This led to the need for something that represented value for everyone.

Over time, certain items began to be used as a common means of exchange, like salt – an essential item that was hard to find in some regions. Eventually, items like precious metals and minted coins were introduced because they were practical, durable, and widely accepted as symbols of value.

The Money We Know Today

As civilizations grew, governments began to issue coins and paper notes, creating the concept of "fiat money" – the money we know today, which represents value but has no intrinsic worth. In other words, a piece of paper or a number in your bank account only has value because we trust that it represents purchasing power.

Nowadays, we don't think twice about the value of the "real" money in our wallets or bank accounts, but it's still just a representation of value based on trust.

And What About Bitcoin?

Like traditional money, Bitcoin is also a representation of value.

The difference is that it isn't issued by a central authority but is instead created and exchanged directly between people through a decentralized, secure network called blockchain. The value of Bitcoin, ultimately, is a matter of trust: it has value because people believe in its worth and the potential of this new technology.

So, What is Real? If something is valuable because people agree it is, then money – whether paper, a digital number, or even Bitcoin – is "real" as long as it has exchange value. Just as salt, gold, and paper money were once accepted as currency, Bitcoin and other cryptocurrencies are becoming a new form of value for many people.

The Future: Exchange Value is What Matters

The truth is that the world will increasingly rely on what holds exchange value. Whether Bitcoin is a scam depends only on the trust people place in it. Just as traditional money has evolved over time, we're witnessing a new stage: the digitalization of value.

So, perhaps the question isn't whether Bitcoin is a scam, but whether we're ready to trust in a new system that reflects the same truth that has always existed – value is whatever people agree has exchange value.

Bitcoin: From Pizza to Power

Imagine a world where money isn't controlled by banks or governments, but by the people. That's the bold idea behind Bitcoin, the first decentralized digital currency. Born in 2008, during a global financial crisis, Bitcoin emerged as a response to the broken trust in traditional systems. Created by the mysterious Satoshi Nakamoto, its goal was simple yet revolutionary: to let people exchange value directly, securely, and without middlemen.

In its early days, Bitcoin was a playground for tech geeks. In 2010, one brave soul used 10,000 BTC to buy two pizzas—a move that made history and probably gave him the most expensive craving ever. As its blockchain technology—essentially a digital ledger that's secure and transparent—gained traction, Bitcoin started making waves beyond the tech bubble.

Fast forward a few years, and Bitcoin had its glow-up. From hitting $1,000 in 2013 to becoming a serious contender in the financial world, it's now embraced by companies, investors, and even countries like El Salvador, where it's legal tender.

But Bitcoin isn't just about numbers going up—it's about challenging the status quo. It's inspired a wave of innovation, like decentralized finance (DeFi) and non-fungible tokens (NFTs), while sparking debates about energy use and regulation.

Today, Bitcoin is no longer the quirky digital experiment it once was. It's a symbol of financial freedom, a tool for innovation, and proof that even in a world of traditional systems, a little rebellion can change everything. And let's be honest—who doesn't love a good underdog story?

Safely Acquiring Bitcoin

1 . Choose a Trusted Exchange

2 . Start by selecting a reputable platform to buy Bitcoin. Look for exchanges with a strong track record, high security, and user-friendly interfaces. Popular options include:

Coinbase: Ideal for beginners, with a simple setup process.

Binance: Offers a wide range of cryptocurrencies and advanced features.

Kraken: Known for its security and diverse payment options.

3. Set Up Your Account

4. Create an account with the chosen exchange.

5. Verify your identity (most exchanges require ID and proof of address for security).

6. Enable two-factor authentication (2FA) for an extra layer of protection.

7. Add Funds

Deposit money into your exchange account using bank transfers, credit cards, or payment apps (depending on the platform).

Be cautious of fees, as some payment methods may have higher charges.

8 . Buy Bitcoin

Navigate to the "Buy Bitcoin" section.

Enter the amount you wish to purchase (most exchanges allow you to buy fractions of Bitcoin).

Confirm the transaction.

Congratulations, you now own Bitcoin!

Safely Storing your Bitcoin

Now that you have Bitcoin, the next step is to keep it safe. You don't want to leave it on the exchange for too long—it's like keeping all your cash in an unlocked drawer.

Types of Wallets

1. A Bitcoin wallet is where your private keys (access to your Bitcoin) are stored. There are two main types:

2. Hot Wallets (Online Wallets)

These are connected to the internet, making them convenient for frequent trading.

Examples: Trust Wallet, Exodus, or wallets integrated into exchanges.

Best for: Small amounts of Bitcoin you plan to trade or spend.

3. Cold Wallets (Offline Wallets)

These are not connected to the internet, making them highly secure against hacks.

Examples: Hardware wallets like Ledger or Trezor.

Best for: Large amounts of Bitcoin or long-term storage.

Setting Up Your Wallet

Download or purchase your preferred wallet.

Write down your seed phrase (a recovery phrase of 12–24 words). Store it offline in a safe place; if you lose this, you lose access to your Bitcoin.

Transfer your Bitcoin from the exchange to your wallet using your wallet's public address.

Pro Tips for Maximum Security

1. Double-Check Addresses: Always confirm the wallet address before transferring Bitcoin to avoid sending it to the wrong place.

Beware of Phishing: Only use official websites and apps to access your exchange or wallet.

2. Diversify Your Storage: Split your Bitcoin between hot and cold wallets to balance security and accessibility.

By following these steps, you'll have your Bitcoin safely in your possession and stored securely, giving you peace of mind as you explore the world of cryptocurrency.

Strategies for Trading Bitcoin and Making Profit

Trading Bitcoin can be thrilling and profitable, but it requires the right strategies and discipline to succeed.

Here's a beginner-friendly guide to understanding and applying the main approaches to Bitcoin trading.

1. HODL (Hold On for Dear Life):

A Long-Term Investment

HODLing is the simplest and most popular strategy among Bitcoin enthusiasts. It involves buying Bitcoin and holding it over the long term, betting on its value increasing with time.

- How it Works:
    - Accumulate Bitcoin gradually, especially during market dips.

- ○ Hold onto it for months or even years.
- ○ Set a clear financial goal, such as saving for a car or a house, and sell only when Bitcoin's value aligns with that goal.
- Best for: Beginners and those with a long-term mindset who believe in Bitcoin's potential.

2. Day Trading: Quick Profits from Market Movements

Day trading is for those who enjoy actively monitoring the market and profiting from Bitcoin's frequent price swings. This strategy requires time, focus, and knowledge of technical analysis.

How it Works:

Buy and sell Bitcoin within a single day, aiming to profit from small price movements.

Use tools like candlestick charts and indicators to predict trends.

Set stop-loss orders to minimize risks if the market moves against you.

Best for: Experienced traders who can dedicate time to watching the market.

3. Swing Trading: Medium-Term Opportunities

Swing trading is ideal for those who don't want the intensity of day trading but still want to benefit from larger price swings over days or weeks.

How it Works:

Analyze the market for entry points, such as buying during dips and selling during peaks.

Hold your position for days or weeks, depending on the trend.

Use both technical and fundamental analysis to make informed decisions.

Best for: Traders who want a balanced approach between active and passive trading.

4. Scalping: High-Frequency Small Trades

Scalping involves making numerous small trades within a day, profiting from minor price changes. It's a high-intensity strategy that demands precision.

How it Works:

Enter and exit trades quickly, often within minutes.

Use leverage (carefully) to amplify gains from small movements.

Focus on high-liquidity markets to execute trades rapidly.

Best for: Advanced traders with experience and access to fast trading tools.

5. Arbitrage Trading: Profiting from Price Differences

Arbitrage trading involves taking advantage of price discrepancies between exchanges. For example, Bitcoin might be priced slightly lower on one exchange and higher on another.

How it Works:

Monitor multiple exchanges for price gaps.

Buy on the lower-priced platform and sell on the higher-priced one.

Factor in fees to ensure profitability.

Best for: Traders with access to multiple exchanges and fast transaction speeds.

General Tips for Trading Bitcoin

1 . Set Clear Goals: Whether you're trading actively or earning passively, define what you want to achieve.

2 . Diversify Strategies: You can combine HODLing, trading, and lending for a balanced approach.

3. Stay Informed: Keep up with market news and technological developments in Bitcoin and DeFi.

Bitcoin trading offers a variety of paths, from hands-on strategies like day trading and arbitrage to passive income through lending and liquidity. Choose the approach that aligns with your financial goals and comfort level, and remember: patience and knowledge are your best allies in this journey.

Passive Income: Lending and Liquidity

If you prefer earning while holding Bitcoin, you can explore passive income opportunities through lending or providing liquidity.

1. Lending:

Platforms like BlockFi, Nexo, or Celsius allow you to lend your Bitcoin to others in exchange for interest payments.

Interest rates can vary but often provide a steady, passive return.

2. Providing Liquidity:

In decentralized finance (DeFi), you can supply Bitcoin to liquidity pools in platforms like Aave or Compound.

You earn rewards or fees for contributing to the liquidity of these ecosystems.

CAUTION: Both options carry risks, such as platform reliability or market volatility, so choose wisely and **DYOR** or

"DO YOUR OWN RESEARCH"

☐ SET CLEAR GOALS

DECIDE WHAT YOU'RE TRADING FOR:
☐ *"IS IT TO BUY A CAR, A HOUSE, OR GROW YOUR SAVINGS?"*

HAVING A CLEAR PURPOSE KEEPS YOU FOCUSED AND MOTIVATED.

☐ DIVERSIFY STRATEGIES

COMBINE METHODS TO SPREAD YOUR RISK:
☐ HODLING FOR LONG-TERM GAINS.
☐ SWING TRADING FOR MEDIUM-TERM OPPORTUNITIES.
☐ LENDING OR LIQUIDITY FOR PASSIVE INCOME.

☐ STAY INFORMED

KEEP UP WITH:
- MARKET NEWS AND BITCOIN DEVELOPMENTS.
- PRICE TRENDS AND TECHNICAL ANALYSIS.
- INNOVATIONS IN DEFI AND BLOCKCHAIN.

☐ MANAGE RISK

ONLY INVEST WHAT YOU CAN AFFORD TO LOSE.

USE TOOLS LIKE STOP-LOSS ORDERS TO LIMIT POTENTIAL LOSSES.

☐ BE PATIENT

BITCOIN IS VOLATILE—DON'T LET EMOTIONS GUIDE YOUR DECISIONS.

REMEMBER, **TIME IN THE MARKET** OFTEN BEATS TRYING TO PERFECTLY "TIME THE MARKET."

Cripto can turn you millionaire

but first will turn you free!

So have fun!

Glossary

1. Bitcoin (BTC):

A decentralized digital currency that operates on a peer-to-peer network, enabling direct transactions without the need for intermediaries like banks.

2. Blockchain:

A secure, transparent, and immutable digital ledger that records all Bitcoin transactions across a decentralized network.

3. Fiat Money:

Traditional government-issued currency, such as the US Dollar or Euro, that has value because it is backed by trust rather than intrinsic worth.

4. HODL:

A slang term in the crypto community meaning "Hold On for Dear Life." It refers to holding onto Bitcoin for the long term, despite market volatility.

5. Day Trading:

A trading strategy where Bitcoin is bought and sold within a single day to profit from short-term price movements.

6. Swing Trading:

A medium-term trading strategy that takes advantage of Bitcoin's price swings over days or weeks.

7. Scalping:

A high-frequency trading strategy that aims to make small profits from numerous trades within a short timeframe.

8. Arbitrage Trading:

A strategy that involves buying Bitcoin at a lower price on one exchange and selling it at a higher price on another to profit from price differences.

9. Hot Wallet:

An online Bitcoin wallet connected to the internet, convenient for frequent trading but more vulnerable to hacks.

10. Cold Wallet:

An offline Bitcoin wallet, such as a hardware wallet, used for securely storing Bitcoin long-term.

11. Liquidity:

The ease with which an asset like Bitcoin can be bought or sold in the market without significantly affecting its price.

12. Lending:

The act of loaning your Bitcoin to others through platforms in exchange for interest, a way to generate passive income.

13. Stop-Loss Order:

A tool used by traders to automatically sell Bitcoin when its price drops to a predetermined level, limiting potential losses.

14. Volatility:

The degree of variation in Bitcoin's price over time, which creates both opportunities and risks for traders.

15. DeFi (Decentralized Finance):

A financial ecosystem built on blockchain technology that enables lending, borrowing, and trading without traditional intermediaries.

16. Private Key:

A secure code that allows access to and control over your Bitcoin. It must be kept confidential, as losing it means losing access to your funds.

17. Seed Phrase:

A series of 12–24 words used to recover your Bitcoin wallet. This phrase should be stored securely offline.

18. Peer-to-Peer (P2P):

A decentralized system where transactions occur directly between users without the need for intermediaries.

19. Market Cap:

Short for Market Capitalization, it represents the total value of all Bitcoin in circulation, calculated by multiplying the current price by the total supply.

20. Satoshi:

The smallest unit of Bitcoin, equal to 0.00000001 BTC. Named after Bitcoin's mysterious creator, Satoshi Nakamoto.

References and Bibliography

- Nakamoto, S. (2008). Bitcoin: A Peer-to-Peer Electronic Cash System. Retrieved from https://bitcoin.org/bitcoin.pdf

- Antonopoulos, A. M. (2017). Mastering Bitcoin: Unlocking Digital Cryptocurrencies. O'Reilly Media.

- A comprehensive guide to Bitcoin's underlying technology and use cases.

- Popper, N. (2016). Digital Gold: Bitcoin and the Inside Story of the Misfits and Millionaires Trying to Reinvent Money. Harper.

- Chronicles Bitcoin's origins and its early adopters.

- Yermack, D. (2013). Is Bitcoin a Real Currency? An Economic Appraisal. NBER Working Paper Series.

- Retrieved from https://www.nber.org/papers/w19747
- Analyzes Bitcoin's economic characteristics and challenges.

- PWC. (2021). Cryptocurrency and its Impact on the Financial Industry.

Retrieved from https://www.pwc.com

- A report on cryptocurrency trends and adoption.

- Binance Academy. (n.d.). What is HODL?. Retrieved from https://academy.binance.com

- Explanation of common cryptocurrency trading terms.

- BlockFi. (n.d.). How to Earn Interest on Your Bitcoin. Retrieved from https://blockfi.com

- Insights into passive income strategies like lending Bitcoin.

- DeFi Pulse. (n.d.). Decentralized Finance (DeFi) Overview. Retrieved from https://defipulse.com

- Information on DeFi platforms and their relationship with Bitcoin.

- Coinbase. (n.d.). How to Store Your Cryptocurrency Safely. Retrieved from https://www.coinbase.com

- A beginner-friendly guide to secure storage options for Bitcoin.

- Woo, W. (n.d.). On-Chain Analysis for Bitcoin Investors. Retrieved from https://woobull.com

- Resources on understanding Bitcoin price trends through blockchain data.

"Take Your First Steps Into the World

Of Bitcoin Trading"

Are you ready to explore the revolutionary world of Bitcoin but don't know where to start? Trading Bitcoin for Doomies! From

Earth to Moon! is your ultimate beginner's guide to mastering Bitcoin trading. Whether you want to grow your savings, achieve financial independence, or simply understand how cryptocurrencies work, this book has you covered.

- Learn how to buy Bitcoin safely and store it securely.

- Discover simple trading strategies that work for everyone.

- Understand the basics of long-term investing (HODL) and how to set financial goals.

- Explore real-world examples to turn knowledge into action.

With clear explanations, engaging examples, and a fun approach, this book makes Bitcoin trading accessible to everyone. Perfect for those new to cryptocurrency or seasoned traders looking for fresh insights, this guide will help you take off on your journey to financial freedom.

There are things we can do the easy way, and then there's crypto — it's not exactly simple!

But don't worry, with this straightforward manual, you'll find some valuable tips to help you dive into this world. Just remember, this isn't financial advice!

Frank

www.ingramcontent.com/pod-product-compliance
Lightning Source LLC
Chambersburg PA
CBHW070125230526
45472CB00004B/1425